Fiddles on the Mountain

Lively Folk Duets for Two Violins

Book One

Myanna Harvey

Cover Image
The Three Tetons, Rocky Mountains, Wyoming - engraving black and white 1898 stock illustration

CHP443

©2024 C. Harvey Publications®
All Rights Reserved.
www.charveypublications.com - print books & free sheet music blog
www.learnstrings.com - downloadable books & chamber music

Fiddles on the Mountain, Book One

Table of Contents

All arrangements by Myanna Harvey

	Page
Kilgary Mountain	2
Kesh Jig	4
Waltzing Matilda	6
The Minstrel Boy	8
Shady Grove	10
Garryowen	12
Sí Bheag, Sí Mhór	14
Temperance Reel	16
The Road to Lisdoonvarna	18
Petronella	20
Wild Mountain Thyme	22
Bill Cheatham	24
Butterfly Jig	26
She Moved Through the Faire	28
Cold Frosty Morning	30
Lady Anne Montgomery	32
Bonaparte Crossing the Rockies	34

About the Duets

Fiddles on the Mountain for Two Violins, Fiddles on the Mountain for Two Violas, and *Fiddles on the Mountain for Two Cellos* are compatible: the parts in these books can also be played as duets with any combination of violin, viola, and cello.

Fiddles on the Mountain: Duets for Two Violins, Book One

Kilgary Mountain

Traditional, arr. M. Harvey

©2024 C. Harvey Publications® All Rights Reserved.

Fiddles on the Mountain: Duets for Two Violins, Book One

©2024 C. Harvey Publications® All Rights Reserved.

Kesh Jig

Trad., arr. M. Harvey

Fiddles on the Mountain: Duets for Two Violins, Book One

©2024 C. Harvey Publications® All Rights Reserved.

Waltzing Matilda

M. Cowan, arr. M. Harvey

©2024 C. Harvey Publications® All Rights Reserved.

Fiddles on the Mountain: Duets for Two Violins, Book One

©2024 C. Harvey Publications® All Rights Reserved.

The Minstrel Boy

Trad., arr. M. Harvey

Fiddles on the Mountain: Duets for Two Violins, Book One

Shady Grove

Trad., arr. M. Harvey

Fiddles on the Mountain: Duets for Two Violins, Book One

Garryowen

Trad., arr. M. Harvey

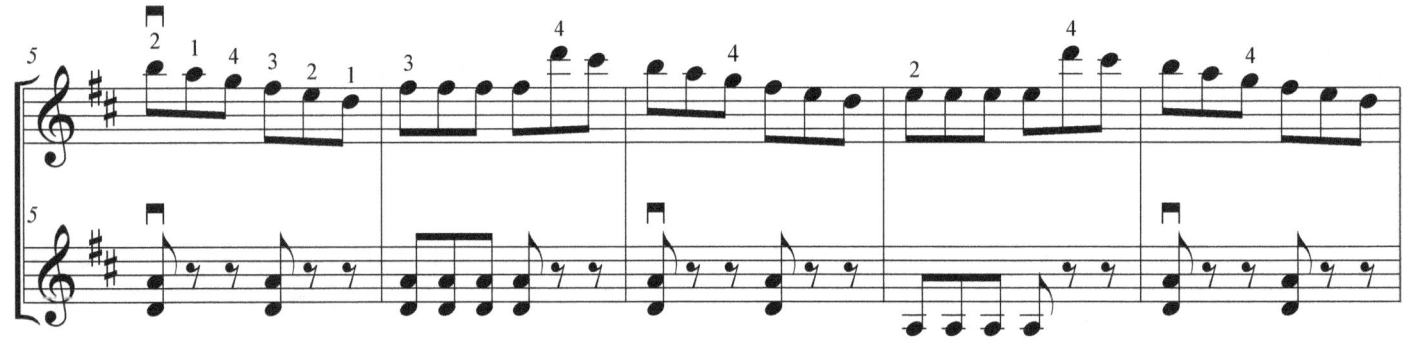

Fiddles on the Mountain: Duets for Two Violins, Book One

13

©2024 C. Harvey Publications® All Rights Reserved.

Sí Bheag, Sí Mhór

T. O'Carolan, arr. M. Harvey

Fiddles on the Mountain: Duets for Two Violins, Book One

15

Temperance Reel

Trad., arr. M. Harvey

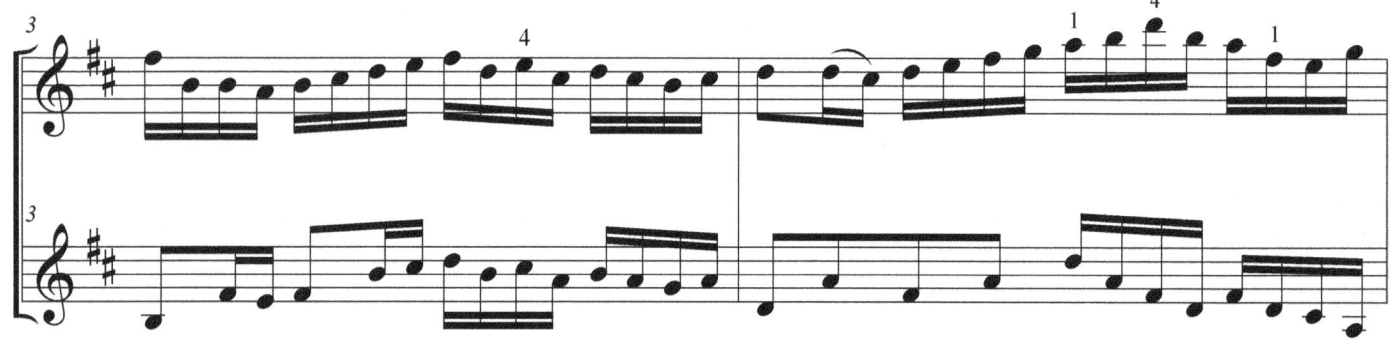

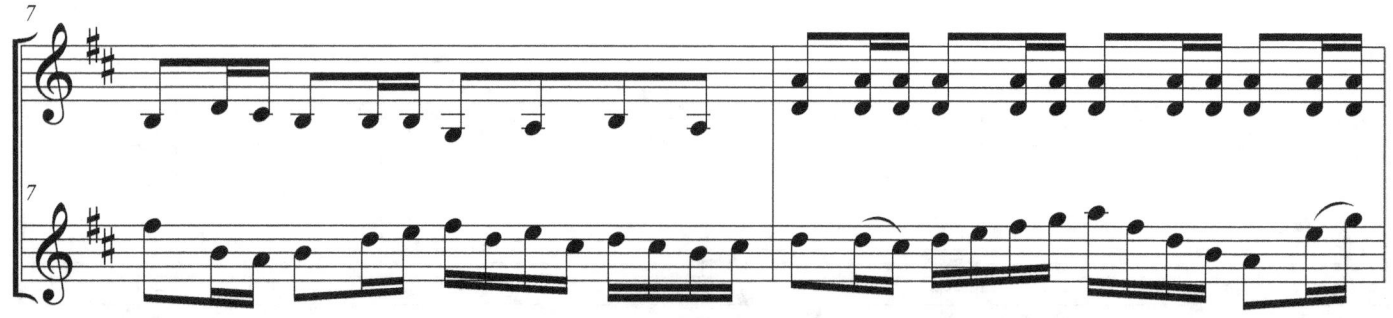

Fiddles on the Mountain: Duets for Two Violins, Book One

©2024 C. Harvey Publications® All Rights Reserved.

The Road to Lisdoonvarna

Trad., arr. M. Harvey

Fiddles on the Mountain: Duets for Two Violins, Book One

19

©2024 C. Harvey Publications® All Rights Reserved.

Petronella

Trad., arr. M. Harvey

Fiddles on the Mountain: Duets for Two Violins, Book One

Wild Mountain Thyme

Trad., arr. M. Harvey

Fiddles on the Mountain: Duets for Two Violins, Book One

©2024 C. Harvey Publications® All Rights Reserved.

Bill Cheatham

Trad., arr. M. Harvey

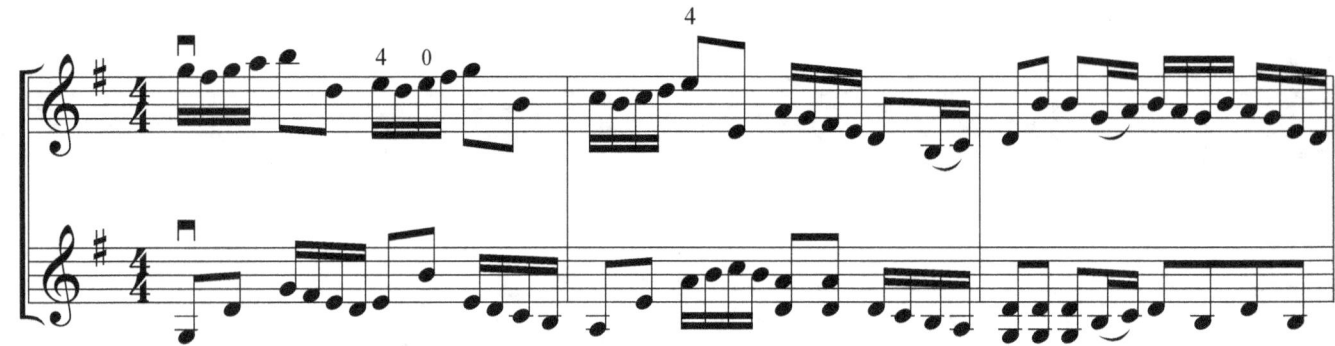

Fiddles on the Mountain: Duets for Two Violins, Book One

©2024 C. Harvey Publications® All Rights Reserved.

Butterfly Jig

Trad., arr. M. Harvey

Fiddles on the Mountain: Duets for Two Violins, Book One

©2024 C. Harvey Publications® All Rights Reserved.

She Moved Through the Faire

Trad., arr. M. Harvey

Fiddles on the Mountain: Duets for Two Violins, Book One

©2024 C. Harvey Publications® All Rights Reserved.

Cold Frosty Morning

Trad., arr. M. Harvey

Fiddles on the Mountain: Duets for Two Violins, Book One 31

Lady Anne Montgomery

Trad., arr. M. Harvey

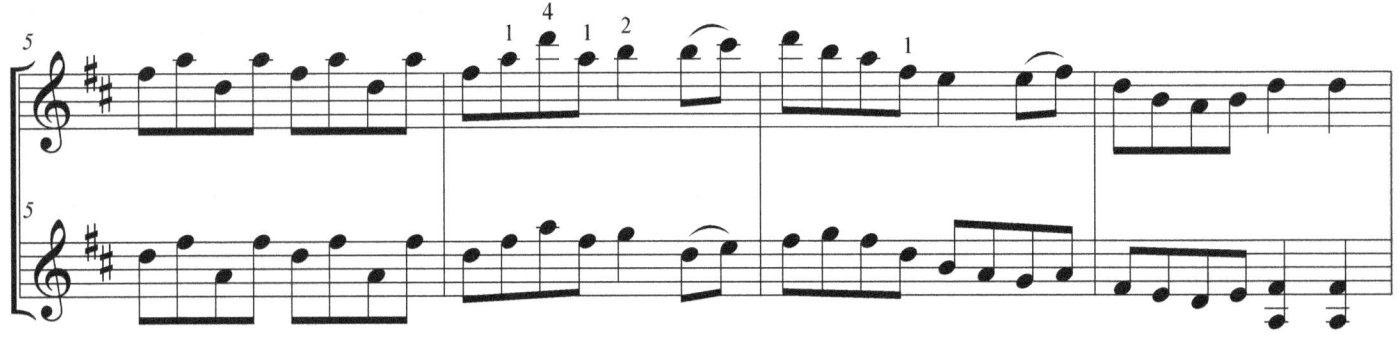

Fiddles on the Mountain: Duets for Two Violins, Book One

©2024 C. Harvey Publications® All Rights Reserved.

Bonaparte Crossing the Rockies

Trad., arr. M. Harvey

Fiddles on the Mountain: Duets for Two Violins, Book One

35

©2024 C. Harvey Publications® All Rights Reserved.

Available from www.charveypublications.com
Dancing Into Bethlehem: Compatible Christmas Duets for Strings

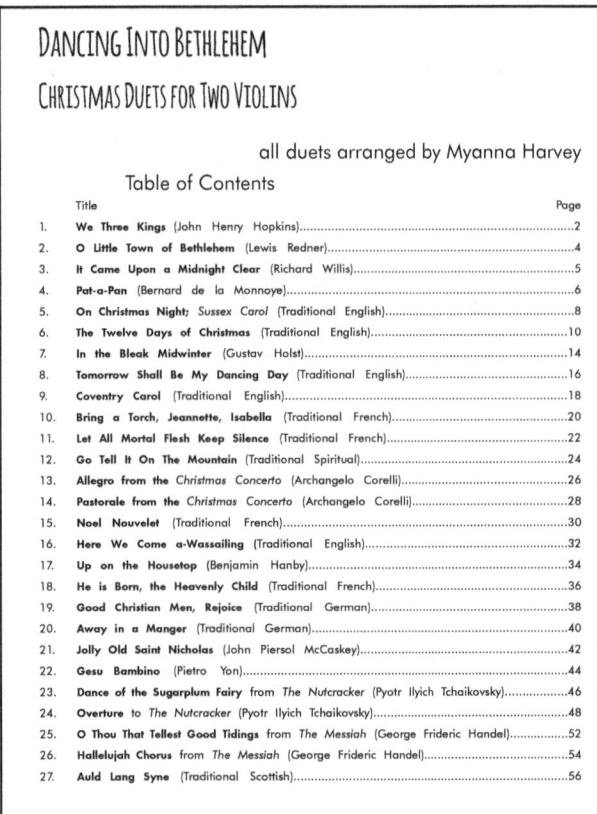

CHP360

CHP361

CHP362